Clara Is Left Out

A Book about Bullying and Kindness

by Kerry Dinmont

Published by The Child's World®
1980 Lookout Drive • Mankato, MN 56003-1705
800-599-READ • www.childsworld.com

Photographs ©: Wave Break Media/Shutterstock Images, cover, 1, 3, 11, 12–13, 14–15, 16; Tom Wang/Shutterstock Images, 4–5; Syda Productions/ Shutterstock Images, 6–7; Danie Nel/Shutterstock Images, 9; Shutterstock Images, 18-19; Digital Vision/Thinkstock, 21

ISBN 9781503820241
LCCN 2016960943

Printed in the United States of America
PA02340

Ava is **bullying** Clara. It makes Clara feel sad.

3

Why should people
be kind?

It is recess. Some kids play tag. Clara wants to play, too.

Ava tells Clara she can't play. Ava is mean to Clara a lot.

Clara is left out. This hurts Clara's feelings.

Mark does not like what Ava did. At lunch, he asks Clara to sit with him.

Clara is happy when she is included.

Mark is happy to include his friend.

Friends do kind things for one another. They can help when you are sad or have a problem.

How did you show **kindness** today?

Glossary

bullying (BULL-ee-ing) Bullying is being mean to someone over and over again. Ava is bullying Clara.

kindness (KIND-ness) Kindness is to be nice to someone. Mark showed Clara kindness by asking her to sit with him.

Extended Learning Activities

1. What kind things do you do for others?

2. Has someone ever made you feel left out? What did they do or say?

3. Have you ever seen anyone being bullied? How could you have stepped in to make that person feel better?

Books

Gilman, Grace. *Dixie and the Big Bully*.
New York, NY: Harper, 2013.

Parr, Todd. *Be Who You Are*. New York, NY:
Little, Brown Books for Young Readers, 2016.

Web Sites

Visit our Web site for links about bullying and kindness:
childsworld.com/links

Note to Parents, Teachers, and Librarians: We routinely verify our Web links to make sure
they are safe and active sites. So encourage your readers to check them out!

About the Author

Kerry Dinmont is a children's book author who enjoys art and nature. She lives in Montana with her two Norwegian elkhounds.